She Will Allow Her Wings

Jane Bluett

[signature: Jane Bluett]

for the LMHT
at Highbury Hospital.
for all their support
and love.

Five Leaves Publications

For Jo and Nick

To lose one great love may be regarded as a misfortune; to lose two looks like carelessness.

Contents

She Will Allow Her Wings
Jane Bluett

Published in 2023 by Five Leaves Publications
14a Long Row, Nottingham NG1 2DH
www.fiveleaves.co.uk
www.fiveleavesbookshop. co.uk

ISBN: 978-1-915434-09-8

Printed in Great Britain

Almah

When I was a young girl, I spoke Hebrew.
I was happy in my words and in my husband,
the writer. It was he saw I was happy,
wrapped me up, wrote me down.

And so they came to read me, translate, interpret.
In Greece my reputation grew as large as my belly.
I was no longer a woman of my world.
My words were mapped by men of letters.

In England they changed the colour of my skin,
wrote in whispers, gave me a sister.
I became the great impossibility,
and she, the other me, a silent whore.

Almah is the Hebrew word meaning 'young girl' used to describe Mary in the Bible. It
attracted connotations of virginity when translated into Greek.

Nushu

With womanwords we made articulate kisses
to the secret ears of sisters.
Our girlish grammar, fierce as flesh, grew strong,
insistent tongues, vital fingers, clawed the taste of talk.
Our nouns slipped silent. our verbs deafened,
loud as sirens, loud as words.

The sentence of our song soared
high enough for girls to reach,
a silky kite of sound, untethered.
And now as I hold language in my arms,
her breath betrays our meaning,
disappears.

Yang Huanyi, the last surviving fluent user of Nushu, the world's only single sex
language, a writing system that for centuries gave voice to the suffering of the female
population of Hunan, China, died in September 2004. Nu Shu means women's writing.

Mary Gives Advice on Contraception

It's best not to talk to strangers in the dark.
Avoid spirits and men called Gabriel.
If you get caught out
reinvent yourself
like Madonna

like a virgin.

Confirmation

At four I saw the big girls
taking bread, asked why
and was told off by nuns
who said I had to draw boys burning.

'Were there dinosaurs in the Garden of Eden?'
The nuns didn't much care for dinosaurs.
The nuns gripped sticks. One afternoon
I had to crawl across a table.

Every fishy Friday we walked back from church,
careful of the lines.
It must have worked,
I never married.

At eleven, in another school,
a teacher asked, 'What religion are you?'
I hardly knew but remembered the bread,
the smells, the bells, and hell.

A Catholic.
'Am I, Mummy, am I?'
The slap of my mother's face said all.
This was my fall, she had to confess.

There would be no white lace dress,
no wine, no transubstantiation,
just guilt, by the gut full,
for ever and ever amen.

Beside the Seaside

Oh you do. Gas rigs twinkle blue, reflect
the carnage at my feet. Hard promenade,
the great Victorian front of Blackpool.
Cold tart, she's pricked by a creaking mast, red
rust, no sail. Sharp wind pierces family
fun. Elephants and wurlitzers squeal: pink
candy, unflossed teeth, grey trunks, DSS
wildlife. A real field of chips and bingo,
slots of fun, prize every time. Sanded down,
the tarnished mile is empty, spent, cashed up
on the shore with cream cones and condoms. I
will leave her a full fat word, a wave of
breath, a small wet death, five for a pound sound,
fresh, wrapped and boxed for a safe journey. Home.

Breaking the Waves

Low tide is cold.
Quiet folds and licks become sand.
A steady foothold shifts.

She is alone tonight by Victorian railings.
Blue paint peels and seagulls mock sound,
steal her voice as she is swept away.

At high tide, waves boom, become sea.
Now the moon might drown the world
in a lunatic flood.

Blackpool's book is unread,
and she has written it in sand
to illiterate, barking seagulls.

When the sun shines as bright as death,
sand burns her feet.
The silent shingle moulds itself to the soul.

Protected Sex

It was always there.
The potential child,
like an imaginary friend,
somewhere behind adolescence.
In the shadow of first cravings
it followed the blood.

When Mandy did it,
took a stand one night
and pushed it out as loud as a playground,
she opened up the can of words:
screw, shag, slut, slag, slut, shag, screw, slag.
A messy business.

So we replied. Pill,
cap, clumsy condom.
The trouble stopped. Our condition
shifted. Would. Should. Could. We were safe,
safe from the clutch of the clinic,
childproof as bottles.

Queer

Little Girl, with curly hair, did what she was told.
Her mother said 'What's on your head is worth its weight in gold.'
Little Girl thought this was cool,
that was, until she went to school.
When the boys came out to play
she had to hide her curls away.
With hat on head she thought she'd try
to kiss the girls but made them cry.
Later, when her head was shaven,
Little Girl became quite brazen,
kissed the boys with pretty faces,
lads with lippy in all the right places.
At last she grew bored with puppy dogs' tails,
so she sliced them off with immaculate nails.
Finally free, with a blonde on each arm,
she knew that her treasure was safe from harm.

Ophelia at the Clinic

I have the daughter's disease, a diseased
daughter, always too close to the water
and slightly hysterical. Or so they
say. I like to put it another way.
When a girl reaches a certain age, a
certain stage in her life, she craves a bit
of excitement. Stuck at home with Father,
who watches every move you make, you take
the first opportunity. The boy next door,
had the looks, read books, talked me into it.
Big mistake. He had his cake, promptly packed
his bags, and went to sea. No thought of me.
Of course I'm hysterical. Stuck in this
place for hours. At least there are flowers.

Stations of the Very Cross

The nun on the bus,
in blue, was beatific.
I sat at the back
in black.

I confessed
to the therapist
who was Irish,
silent, unforgiving.

Cousin Peter got fat
in Rome. He came home
to be adored,
to perform marriages.

Uncle Ray, the doctor,
was gay.
He swapped Ireland
for the Emerald City.

Aunt Bid who escaped
the Poor Clares,
took on airs. She spoke
to the gods in the sink.

Granny had a sacred heart.
She took us to masses
at lightning speed
in Latin.

In the seventies
Popes died like rabbits
and Elvis.
Men in frocks.

And how shall you be,
my child,
when you choose to sleep
with a ghost?

Eat chocolate,
watch the clouds
all Easter Sunday,
waiting.

When he finally came
I uttered his name
too loudly.
They locked me away.

Mary, Mary,
quite contrary,
which one shall you be?
It's Magdalene for me.

How do they pronounce
that in Oxford?
The Lord's Prayer
has two endings.

One, where our father
swears at the tomb
of the Bishop of Dublin.
Sweet Jesuit!

Another, where a mother
weeps for a dead boy.
Pieta.
Cold hard stone.

Sibling Rivalry

In Wamena, Indonesia
my brother lives with ancient men,
fruit gatherers who celebrate the dead in vivid colours.
Above the trees, above the rain,
he prays for peace in a language I will never understand.
He sends me pictures to click and save.

In Nottingham, England,
I watch my garden from the first floor window.
The apple tree sighs as its fruit drops.
I cannot rescue fruit,
but I can read the words of ancient men,
write the death of apples.

Where the Clever Women Are

The good lecturer talks about signposts
through fresh printed pages that turn in new
directions. This woman talks it easy
but the fresh map in her clever mouth is
not there nor here. Each contour disappears
as it is spoken, horizons vanish.
Her words are impossible to manage,
their co-ordinates smudge my page. Muddy
footprints ask me, 'Have we been here before?'
At half past four, she folds the world away.
On my own two feet again, I stumble,
but decide to follow the breadcrumbs home,
where my mother will mend my map for me,
certain, fixed and plotted from A to B.

Hamlet's Big Sister

We heard the news in England.
Your insane attempt at family
therapy failed. I said it would,
but no one listened.
You were all talk, no action.

And who voted you Daddy's girl
all of a sudden? When you dished out
the parts, where was mine?
Danish swine. You should have
loved your mother.

She loved you. As most mothers do –
in the knowledge that
they can't compete. When I
left home, I left. No weekend visits
even for funerals,

even to be told that I was fat and wheezing
from the fags. *That's what happens to
drunken slags*, you said.
And now you're dead. Who
will clean your messes now?

Not me, sweetheart brother. I will not
be your mother or her daughter.
My broken crown will mend alone
with words, written, unheard.
I'll write of you in England.

Outsider

I am outside.
A lock that will not give
sucks time through its cold mouth.
The locksmith turns the hole to wood shavings.

I am outside.
On a tiled threshold time turns tight.
The locksmith splits cold rigid steel.
He picks and pushes, expert.

I am outside.
He is in.

Dear Mr Larkin

I think I met you once at a station.
I remember your inch-thick specs,
your large hands ungloved,
the receding hairline.
You talked to my friend,
they all did in the end,
as I waltzed off in nylons
and shoes *à la mode*.
I never read books but loved the jazz,
the dudes, their smiles, their talk,
up close and personal.
They loved the fur, the bosomy sax,
the dark, grunting silence.
Had I met you twice I might have smiled.
I'm not someone to talk to.
With your inch-thick specs
you might have thought me beautiful.

Breast Flasher Jailed for Assault, Brighton 2006

Intelligent woman with issues
flashes her tits in a bar.
Glorious vodka-filled tits
assault the air and the other drinkers,
who prefer their tits passive.
She cries 'Here they are, arrest them.
take them in, send them down.
They will spit in the mouths of children
if you let them.'

Marc Almond's Poodle

A house where people left things,
moments, Mondays, memories,
a great big shell of a house.

Young divas with make-up thicker than skin
left virginities and STDs upstairs,
the contents of their stomachs in the sink.

Lads with lethal manes of hair,
furtive flamingos,
left brew stains and spliff burns on sheets.

I left my heart every time,
like a marshmallow sacrifice,
no matter how I hardened it.

A few left sanity
in the attic,
the exit was a long way down.

The day Marc Almond left his poodle,
we knew the house was damned
or beautiful.

Beauty Sleep

She often woke up in strange places
with the feeling she'd lost her shoes.
This morning, she was frozen.
She had believed another handsome prince,
fallen for his happy, here, right now, routine.

Hair spilled down the side of someone's bed,
her crimson mouth lay quiet, she dared not breathe.
In this glass tomb, she would lie still, white as ice
for as many years as it took the prince
to notice her cold rejection.

Little Red

I was happy in the woods.
The nights were dark as bark,
the clubs were packed with predatory eyes,
intent on the chase, the game, the good time.
It always ended the same,
on a bed of needles.
Quite by surprise I left one day.
The trees gave way to a City of Gold
where they gave me credit for everything.
I took taxis through the woods at night
threw small change from the window.
They were dying in the woods.
In the City the lawyer who wed the accountant
lived corporately ever after.
Lies grow fat behind pinstripes,
glass slippers become ceilings.
'Wear a shorter skirt, little girl,
keep the clients happy.'
I wish, I wish, I wish.
No one likes a girl who knows what she wants.
Woodcutters came with clipboards,
cut off my head, filled it with stones
until my mind rattled:
take me back to the woods
to the damaged goods,
take me back to the darkness,
back to the truth,
take me back to the good time,
back to the big bad wolf.

The Little Mermaid

We let you go out on the water that night,
in search of a prince, but the cool kiss
of the Thames, old and trusted father,
who you loved best, stopped your lover's song
with his dark dirty mouth. He took your golden hair
in his filthy fingers and dragged you down
to where the knotted flow of water is neither
loud nor long but silent, where stones
will tear the feet of an angel as she falls.

They dredged you out from the water's shadows,
cut off your hands, cut off your beautiful
little hands, the hands that made the air sing,
on a rooftop, somewhere in the City.
Only the tattoo told us it was you,
we never saw your golden smile again.
A cruel collision at Canon Street Bridge
and then silence, ever, ever after.
Sweet Thames run dry, you have killed your daughter.

Avalanche

It was quiet at first,
a few disturbances at the summit,
small vibrations underfoot.
They noticed that the sun
became unbearably bright,
as bright as blindness.
Birds sang as if life itself were a chorus.
Leaves shivered green
with all the knowledge of the world.
Year upon year of snow

severed itself from its foundations

then the roar.

Postcards

The day the postcards came
wasn't a Tuesday,
it was the middle of much.
First, a seaside pink grotesque
wished I was here.
Then kittens with blue ribbons
greeted me from somewhere else.

One after one they came.
I tried to kill the postman
but they wouldn't stop.
Just drop, drop, drop
onto the not-so-welcome mat.

Postcards from everywhere.
So where was I?
Not where you would wish to be.

Beside the sea?

Beside the sea?

I grabbed one of a donkey in a hat,
looked for my address,
it wasn't there.

It wasn't a Tuesday.
Wish you were here?

Mirror

Are you still here?
In this morning debris I get the sense
of cigarettes, wine and sweat,
something half alive.

Each night, I'll drink you out
to come back to myself.
I'll meet disaster halfway,
be abandoned.

I need to be alone or dead
away from this rejection.
I am as ugly as regret.
Are you still here?

Alice's Tears

A yellow moon is in the sky,
the colour of matchboxes.
It sifts between green curtains,
spills tears into her sleeping head.

As each tear breaks, it speaks.
Wet words are slow, must run to get dry.
Faster, louder, rounder, harder,
mother, brother, sister, father.
A sturdy mast to dry the tears
of the world as she hears it
from the unstable deck of her bed.

When tears are as dry as tinder,
the lifeboats of reason ignite.
She must jump overboard
to save the burning words and swim,
like Alice,
because she can.

Sleeping Beauty

Because you were pricked by a needle,
there was no glass coffin,
just hardwood from the Co-op.
The apple in your throat stuck
as they pushed you into the oven.
There was no wake up kiss.
I cut briars with my heart.

Poor Ghost

I remember first the bowler hatted sight of you
clockwork in the furious city sun.
The breathing leather backcombed nights of you,
when Time had winked and we had just begun.
I remember when I squatted days of you,
we lost our minds like keys and we were one.
We kissed and I drank in the breath of you,
so drunk I knew how games were lost and won.
I remember how I loved the poking bones of you,
your skinny swagger, when the deals were done.
I would have chased the shadow that was left of you,
when Time was called, doors closed, when Time was done.
I remember how I cried to hear the last of you,
and listening for your words, found there were none.

Elegy

To say we weren't the perfect couple
is saying Hamlet's a bit sad.

You in Docs and leather
and me in some flowery number
that covered the bruises.
But we were happy.

As happy as a bottle of JD can make you
on a sunny Hackney afternoon
when intellect is a kicked in telly, a screwed up CV.
But we were happy.

Our love was fucking, fags and futility.
But we were happy.
Somewhere between eruption, eviction and bed.
I miss you now you're dead.

A Day will Come

A day will come when I won't need to write
about you or the things you did and said.
A day will come when all the crap just might
have silenced, flushed the anger from my head.

A day will come when roses that you stole
from graveyards don't burn petals to my eyes.
A day will come when I will feel whole
not left undone by acid truth and lies.

Until that day my words will not ignite
your gorgeous face, cold stone, upon the page.
Until that day when I can pen you right
there's nothing more but love and loss and rage.

Psychogrammar

He sits in that chair every week,
waits for me to speak.
I know his name,
he knows mine
but we never use them.

The silence is taut, I crack:

You know when you get drunk
You know when you get high
You know when you get low
You know when someone dies

He knows all right
but all he's interested in is grammar.

'You know when you talk about you,
you talk about 'you'?'

I do.
And the 'I' sticks in my throat like a first word.
And this is why I hurt.

You know that, don't you?

The Last Session

After all those years, those tears,
For the first time, I touched you.
I shook your hand, made you stand,
took back power.
I talked you my life
for an hour a week.
The assumptions of others,
lovers, brothers, mothers
and here I am shaking
your hand in mine.
Saying goodbye to allocated time.

Four Ways with Words

Shall I speak you?
Mouth your words?
Articulate the air, sound you out.

When I hear you
vibrations roll through me.
I tremble with an inward narrative.

As I read you
eyes move side to side, taking in your show.
Reading is a slow art. No hurry.

When I write you
my pen pulses.
I define your shape. I draft you, let you go.

Living Together

When you said 'we' for the first time
my vegetable heart ripened.
This was not for show.
Your voice had shifted.

I sifted you in
blended you into me
until we were mutual
we shared language.

You may unpick spears
from this artichoke heart
but your words will stay.
Your word, ours.

A Private Place

The sun is busy this morning, trying
to break a window locked against the light.
We lie, cleaved, in month-old sheets, clenched like teeth,
biting the tongues of the darkness. We know
together has no meaning. In the green
half-light, I caress the skull beneath your
skin, bury my burning legs into the
clammy cushion of your night sweat. The sun
has no business here, this is a sour night
that has been a long day in the making.
Too much, too often has brought us to a
bed where suns don't shine, no matter how hard
the window smashes. Together. Tell the
sun to take his fist and chide small children.

A Crow at Blidworth

In the woods, on a well-trodden path,
horses' breath smudges May
as the wind manhandles new buds.
We are walking in our own footsteps.

Suddenly, a crow
reaches out a span of frenzied feathers,
a broken greeting.
Its wing is heavy, black lead.

We are closer now.

The crow cowers in an attempt at flight,
scuttles into unfamiliar grasses.
That huge bird becomes small, lopsided,
ill-equipped for walking.

As we wander towards The Fox and Hounds,
the crow throws its shadow at our feet.
Today we are too close to ourselves,
too close to wring its neck.

Melencolia I

The builders have been in. She sighs.
It is grey twilight. Angel empties her bag.
Her instruments clatter onto old wood that feels no pain.
She slumps into a chair, kicks off the shoes
that bind her feet in public. This is the moment
she would call for the child, if she had one.
The dog hasn't been fed for days, it sleeps thinly.
Angel's humour is black and she laughs to herself.
The dress she wears doesn't suit her, it feels big,
like a man's imagination. The builders have left tools:
slide rule, athanor, set square, pincers, hammer, plane.
Instinct checks her pockets, purse and keys chime,
remind her that the bell is broken.
The room is like a sea, alarmingly calm,
strewn with debris. Her hair itches.
Angel nudges the contents of her bag, indifferent.
She checks the numbers that always add up the same.
They tell her that she is and will be thirty four.
Angel notices the clock has stopped, counts instruments and tools.
Later she will carve her name in thick bloody gouges,
feel at last the crack of her spine and tearing skin.
She will count, swallow hard and scatter the room.
Clawing the manmade fibres of her dress,
she will allow her wings.